Winds of Time

poems by
Ronda Miller

Kellogg Press   Emporia, KS

Also by Ronda Miller

Going Home: Poems from My Life
MoonStain
WaterSigns

Winds of Time
Copyright © 2019 Ronda Miller

All rights reserved. No part of this publication may be reproduced, distributed, or transmitted in any form or by any means, without prior written permission of the publisher.

This is a work of fiction. The names, characters, places, and incidents are either a product of the author's imagination or used fictitiously, and any resemblance to actual persons living or dead, business establishments, events, or locals is entirely coincidental.

Published by Kellogg Press
1114 Commercial St.
Emporia, Kansas 66801
kelloggpress.com

Printed in the United States of America

Curtis Becker, Editor/Layout and Design/Cover Design
curtis@curtisbeckerbooks.com
curtisbeckerbooks.com

Patrick Emerson, Cover Art
lpatrickemerson@att.net
500px.com/patrickemerson
flickr.com/photos/kansasphoto
facebook.com/LPatrickEmerson/

ISBN: 978-0-578-57489-9

Praise for Winds of Time

In every turning clock, there are arrows of time, each a tine that points at moments passed; that can still pierce through today. *Winds of Time* captures these moments as confessionals. Ronda's poetry meditates on, "...a time warp threaded to me/ from a past or future unrealized."

> —Huascar Medina, Poet Laureate of Kansas, 2019-2021, *How to Hang the Moon*

Miller turns dirt into gold, difficulty into transcendence—and does so with such an easy grace that we may not notice its artfulness, its attention to voice, phrase, and stance. There's much to learn here.

> —Kevin Rabas, Poet Laureate of Kansas, 2017-2019, *Watch Your Head*

As scientists continue to explore why time exists, poet Ronda Miller, in Winds of Time, shows time is interwoven with memory. These poems of witness are to remind us we, too, are witnesses. Sometimes it means returning to one's hometown. Family can be a difficult but necessary challenge. Miller shows us how we are dealt hardships even by "Mother Nature's sometimes cruel hand, undeserving..."Sometimes the hardship comes in the form of an uninvited stranger with a needle. Within this dance of struggle and beauty on the Great Plains, Miller triumphantly confesses, "love is my politics." Love is what circles us through time and memory, even as the last line of the collection circles to the first when she explains, "I am from and I go forth." I am thankful to be a reader of this collection to remind myself that a place of being is "a part of the place that birth[s us], into this time."

> —Dennis Etzel, Jr., *This Removed Utopia*

Winds of Time is dedicated to all those who have blown through this earthly existence; past, present, and future.

Apollonia Shreders Racca
Scott Shreders
Gabrial Racca
Nick, Julie, Dimitry Shreders
Sasha Shreders
Scott Wiggins
Jena Acors
Janelle Andrews

Other support relatives and friends too numerous to mention.

Table of Contents

WindsOfTime	1
Hometown	2
Jim Smelled of Danger	3
Anna's Piano	5
Granny Got Eggs	7
Nebraska	9
[deer slain, edge of road]	10
Dad	11
Us Dogs	14
Dragonfly	15
In Utero	17
Pickles	21
Time Zone in Scorpio	22
Life Needs	23
Aberration - Father Time ainhiraf waqt al'ab	25
This Life, This Dance	27
Spirit of America	28
I Am	29

WindsOfTime

Today we ride
the winds of time.
The tines from the wind
won't let us unwind.
They rock us through eternity
in an endless, relentless sea.
They gift us with the music
of love as the tune of wind
blows from high above.

In life's brine
and brackish tide,
we see blue of heaven,
Earth's green hue.
We hitch a ride on dew
of moon to ride
the winds of time again.

The tines from the wind
hold the bite of winter in.
They are overlaid
with memories
of where we are going,
where we have been.

Ronda Miller

Hometown

I rode the winds
of my hometown,
heard the gossip,
became the topic.
I hurried the ground
beneath my feet;
anxious to grow,
to leave,
others had,
most did.
When life's mirror
reflected back,
so many decades past,
memories swayed
from a life hard lived.
Those left in my hometown
had not changed.
My thoughts about
them did. The gossip
I'd heard and caused
was love and concern—
not ill intent.
Curious minds wish
to know those amongst them.
How else may they best serve?
The ground I'd hurried
beneath my feet
felt the same
beneath bare toe.
We breathed as one,
that town and I,
as I grew old.

Winds of Time

Jim Smelled of Danger

but my nose interpreted desire.
He was my sister's
boyfriend from high school.
That was a half decade past and
she was married and pregnant
when he came to visit.

We hadn't seen him
since his junior year of high
school when he shot himself
in the stomach, no accident.
His family left town
as soon as he could travel.

His younger brother, Danny,
was my boyfriend. We
didn't know we needed
to say goodbye.

A few months later, I
tried to run away from home. I
took a photo of Danny with me.

The first empty house
I stayed in, just up the road -
I didn't make it far on foot -
I set fire to that photo.

Soon after, I
heard my boyfriend had burned
to death in a fire. He'd
run back into the house
to get a picture

Ronda Miller

    of someone he loved.

    Jim found me on Facebook
    a month ago. He
    told me my sister still owned
    a piece of his heart. Yesterday,
    Jim sent a photo of Danny. It
    was like the one I'd set fire to.

Winds of Time

Anna's Piano

sits untouched,
takes up space
in my dining room
where most people
have a table,
guests and laughter.
It waits,
as do I.

In a few years Anna
will be old enough
to home the piano
of her childhood. It's
the one her daddy
helped her learn
to play, encouraging
clumsy fingers
that grew long
too quickly, preferring
the feel of reins entwined
between them over
the light touch needed
to play the piano.

Her father insisted
on lessons for music,
dance, and the language
of horses. He'd learned
the patience of love
from previous marriages and
three older sons.

The piano sits silent
knowing I can't bear

Ronda Miller

to hear the sounds
it made when her daddy
was alive. We'd sit together,
he and I,
on the piano bench,
warmed by the afterglow
of our lovemaking.

Anna doesn't know I have
the piano, she doesn't
remember me. I
was the one
who watched from
peripheral sidelines
and waited. I took the piano
when I learned Anna's mother
didn't have room. There
are three other children
in her life with her new husband.

Years die swiftly. One day
I'll give Anna her piano, but
for now I stare at the strong,
solid stance of the piano's legs,
touch the smooth gloss
of the wood that reminds
me of his skin, and find
I'm happy.

Granny Got Eggs

lives in the Airbnb space
connected to my one night
stay in small town Kansas
just east of The Arikaree Breaks.

Granny sees me driving back
and forth, then parked
in the church parking lot
while I check the address
for the tenth time. She
walks out to the 'no excuse
excuse' of a street with a broom
in her hand. I roll down my window,
ask about the address. She
points the broom handle
across the street, tells me,
'park the other side of the pick up',
unlocks the door, gives me a tour.

I sleep the sleep of the dead, dreaming poet. Vivid
dreams of my grandmother, country living,
missing the doings, the comings and goings,
of farm life.

The next morning, granny got eggs
gifts me eggs. We have a gifting war. I
give her books of my poetry, she
states she loves poetry, I suggest
she may not love mine. She replies,
"I'm no Quaker!" as she runs next door
to bring me a newspaper article
displaying a photo of her with friends
from decades past.

Ronda Miller

I drink in the surrounding
buildings. Her eyes follow mine.
She tells me what they used to be,
implies they were somehow
better then than they are now. Like
she could be more perfect.

I start to back my car
out of the lot, she catches
me one last time to gift
a bottle of her homemade
salad dressing.
"Shake it good!" she hollers.

I'll be back,
I just don't know when.

Nebraska

Snow falling on daffodils,
fluffy and light,
a delightful sight, yellow
against white.
Green hues surround,
traffic abounds subdued
by the hues
against the backdrop
of my barn red house. I
allow thoughts to calm,
angst in my heart
these last weeks
knowing the hardship area
neighbors and friends in Nebraska
were dealt by Mother Nature's
sometimes cruel hand, undeserving.
A reminder that seasons
do come, do pass, delicate
flowers survive the blast,
beaten down, will rise,
faces to the sun with
a strength instilled
by the Gods above,
christened by tears.

Ronda Miller

[deer slain, edge of road]

deer slain, edge of road
coyotes run in pack of five
redbuds burst in bloom

Dad

Sometimes you skip
over the things in therapy
that are the reason
you are in therapy.
But the man
standing silently invisible
by the door,
holding his head
in his hands,
is my dad
and he can't speak and
I can't speak,
so I sit through
that session and the next and
the next mute and muted.

I dream of my decapitated
dad, who is the dad
of my childhood
reality even before he died.
His was the face
cut by my grandparents
from the photographs
that included my mom, siblings,
and me.

The headless, fatherly man
was the man who kidnapped
me and moved every month
to keep from getting caught.
We were hungry and scared
and freezing and I got tired
of hearing the beatings

Ronda Miller

of children and women
through paper thin walls,
never knowing,
not knowing,
did they hear mine, too?

But I know he had a head,
he laid it in my lap one time
when I was five and I touched
his beautiful auburn hair,
smoothed it away from his face.

I saw it again at 19,
years after the Kansas
court system decided
Colorado wasn't the place
I should live and that my father
should live in prison for a time.

The last time I saw his head
was in a coffin, after his murder,
but I think it was connected to his body.
I didn't check. I can't be certain.

In my dreams, waking and sleeping,
it is the headless dad I see. He
stabs my grandfather to death
for molesting me.
He looks over my shoulder
as I brush my teeth, appears
in closets and dark, shadowy
bottoms of swimming pools.

Winds of Time

He is always watching
looking out for me,
just as I am always
looking,
watching,
waiting for him
to give me
permission to speak.

Ronda Miller

Us Dogs

I awaken to the sound
of dogs barking in the distance. They
are up early to have a chance
to socialize before sleep
stumbling owners herd them indoors
to begin their own morning routines.
The dogs are out long enough to share
a quick recap of their nights,
"Mama let me sleep in bed, Papa
is away on business."
"I sourced a chicken bone
from the trash last night. Man it was tasty,
but I've been feeling the effects
of those splinters. The pain!"
"Julie is coming home from college!
I'm so excited. I hope she brings
me a special treat!"

So it goes until the last
one has been whistled,
coaxed, cajoled or bribed
into their homes. Quiet
returns, owners attempt
to sleep another precious
few minutes before the sun rises and
their alarms jolt them awake.

Us dogs sleep til' noon.

Winds of Time

Dragonfly

"You can't sit still, can you?"

His voice comes through
as a soft breeze on a hot night titillating/tender.

She fully awakens to a light touch
on her hand, just above
the wedding ring she still wears.
'Believe it, it's him.'

She glances at the clock - 5:35 a.m.
It is the same time daily.

He was always an early
riser, up hours before her,
making coffee, taking
the dog for a walk,
reading the paper, catching
early morning political programs.

The veil so thin, thinner daily,
this illusionary life/death crossover.

She, so desperate to believe, believes.

She glances into the once manicured backyard.
It looks like an English garden now. An unruly,
wild one.

His face hovers
over a flower, glances
in her direction, winks.

Ronda Miller

>The dragonfly he has become
moves swiftly, away from
her line of vision.

In Utero

I
Was
The
Girl
Who
Slept
In
Late
One
Sunny
Fall
Morning
Who
Had
A
Stranger
Walk
Into
My
House
And
Stick
A
Needle
In
My
Arm
For
Three
Days
And
As
Many

Ronda Miller

Nights
The
Needle
Booted
Back
And
Forth
Between
Errands
I
Ran
For
This
Stranger
I
Remember
Little
Else
Except
How
Much
I
Loved
The
High
And
Hated
The
Low
And
How
I
Later
Preferred
Heroine
Over

Winds of Time

The
Speed
He'd
Put
In
My
Veins
I
Never
Shot
Myself
Up
Always
Preferring
Someone
Else
To
Give
The
Pain
And
The
Pleasure
When
Out
Of
Drugs
We
Used
Water
As
It
Was
The
Needle

Ronda Miller

Going
Into
My
Arm
I'd
Fallen
In
Love
With
I
Loved
Feeling
Pain free
Floating
Like
An
Unborn
Child
In
Utero

Pickles

There is a half eaten jar
of pickles in the Walmart
parking lot. Picnic or spilled goods?

He has tats covering his entire body,
well, those parts I can see.
One teardrop descends
from his left eye.

I tell him I like the tats,
wish they were raised
so if I were blind
I could see them
with my hands.

I imagine tracing them
with a forefinger,
tentative at first,
then with an open hand,
welcoming them in.

A dragon, fireflies, flowers,
intricate scrollings
in a multitude of colors
spill onto his neck, arms and
legs. They entwine with each other.

I tell him he should lose the tear,
he looks at me with questioning eyes.

"I can cover it if you'd like?"
"No," I reply, "lose it. You're happy now."

He nods his head in agreement.

Ronda Miller

Time Zone in Scorpio

Fiery ramifications,
a blazing sun.
S. Korean silent,
not to embarrass self,
national communique.

There's something not right
with the sky tonight, hot
breath of summer months
away. Miami man at Swope Park,
slinking rage, scent of murderous ways.

Something's not right
with the sky today,
it's pushing me away.
'It's too bright,
it's not like this every day.'

Breath comes overwrought,
too much afterthought.

'Breathe in, breathe out.'

Something's not right with
the moon tonight, it's purple, not gold.
The squirrel is acting crazed.

'Come inside, darling, it's cold.'

Fingers lace amidst flowers.

Life Needs

My psychiatric days were
laden with pill popping
prescriptions, restraints, meetings
with silent therapists, fending
off the ones who took advantage
of my illnesses. I began
getting into their pants
before they got into
mine, then the realization
that my health
was in my hands
all of that time. My
wellness was
centered on accepting
I could feed
my body, soul and spirit,
with love attained
from all areas of the planet. I
could work with kids, walk
with dogs, meditate
on leaves, forever weave
relationships, each unique
as a fingerprint
or a snowflake, reach out
a hand, meet a stranger's
smile knowing all the while
knowing none of us are strangers.
Not really.
We experience the same
game, some start off on higher
ground, but around and around
we go. We spin and fall, crawl,
walk, then crawl. This life

Ronda Miller

>is so beautiful with so much
>to see, to share with those
>who care. It's learning
>what your body needs. Is
>it calcium and chai seeds? No
>meat on my plate, please.
>Vitamin D and feeling
>the breeze of an early morning
>thunderstorm that strikes
>lightning close enough
>to rock me to my knees, not
>in fear but to say thanks, and
>please, may I experience
>that one more time? I want
>to feel electricity. There,
>that's the extent of humanity,
>to fill each person's needs.
>to feel
>to fill
>to feel
>to fill.

Winds of Time

Aberration - Father Time
ainhiraf waqt al'ab

I see him out of my peripheral
vision, turbaned head, full
graying beard, dark skin,
sandals, wrinkled cotton
clothing unlike what
we generally wear
in American culture.

Most eye catching
is the large dark walnut,
wood framed clock
he carries in place
of a heart.

He's smiling, has a genuine
affable attitude, but then,
he's got time on his side,
within himself.

I imagine the tick
of his clock from where
I spin tires. I do a 180, want,
no, need, to capture him
with a quick photo.

He's gone. I'm disappointed,
appreciate I might have taken
a wrong turn, think maybe
he was an illusion, a mirage.
It is a hot day.

Ronda Miller

        The realization that he
        was a time warp threaded to me
        from a past or future yet unrealized
        abeyance by my conscious state.

        I drive around the block, ask
        people as they pass, "Have
        you seen the middle Eastern
        man carrying the clock?" They
        look at me like I'm crazy, some
        smile, most shake their heads.

This Life, This Dance

love is my politics
I give
I have
I rarely rave
about the world
at large
I live within
my skin is thin
I try not to make things hard
I do not judge
least I too be judged
I have sinned
I have wronged
I continue to sing
my songs
on my death bed
please kiss my head
know the fighting
the wrongs
were righted
the trees
the birds
the bees
clean air
trickling brooks
I've almost done it all
what I haven't seen
this place
the dream
the rest
upon reawakening

Ronda Miller

Spirit of America

was in their eyes
as horse and rider
crossed the countryside.
Fleet of foot
and filled with pride,
carrying mail west
then back to the other side.

Dreams were
laid like railroad ties.
Men looked upwards
and watched the skies
for signs of clouds
and eagle's cries.

Through blizzards, drought,
and decades the hooves still rise.
Just listen for their sounds
as the night wind sighs.

I Am

from NPR prompt "I am from..."

I am from high plateaus,
roving wheatfields, wind
that blows from all directions —
sometimes, all at once.

I am from dirt mixed
with blood, memories
unreachable, unthinkable,
unmistakable human fragility
and strengths cannoned
into one being.

I am from the smell of oil
caked dirt, acrid cattle shit,
snow so fresh the land devours
it in giant gulps that spew
forth mists, inhaled to leave
lungs frostbitten, minds
yearning, listing toward
spring thaw.

I am from creek beds
layered with dinosaur bones,
fossilized cottonwood seeds,
corn tassels, Cheyenne Indian arrowheads, hope.

I am come come come
into being
a part of the place
that birthed me,
into this time.
The fiber of my insides

Ronda Miller

>carry cells regenerated/regenerating
>by generations of eating
>dirt in all its glorious forms.
>
>I am from and I go forth.

About the Author

Ronda Miller does Peer Life Coaching with clients with opioid addictions, with a specialty niche working with clients who have lost someone to homicide. She is a graduate of the University of Kansas and continues to live in Lawrence. She is a Fellow of The Citizen Journalism Academy, World Company, a Certified Life Coach with IPEC (Institute of Professional Empowerment Coaching), a mother to two step sons, Sasha and Nick, a son, Scott, daughter, Apollonia, son-in-law Gabriel, and grandson, Dimitry. She created poetic forms loku and ukol. Miller was the poetry contest manager for Kansas Authors Club (2011-2014), District 2 President of Kansas Authors Club (2015 – 2017), the club's Vice President (2016 – 2017), and state President (2018 - 2019). When Miller isn't coaching clients, volunteering time to Kansas Authors Club, or writing poetry, she is wandering the high plateau of NW Kansas where the Arikaree Breaks scream into blizzards and whisper during thunderstorms. Watch for Miller's other books: *Going Home: Poems from My Life*, *MoonStain*, and *WaterSigns*. Her first illustrated children's book, *I Love the Child*, has an expected release date of 2020, along with her memoir, *Gun Memories*.

Praise for Ronda Miller's Poetry

Miller's poems snap open like a milkweed pod to release their seeds of visceral life, silky from the interior life, to bud and bloom again. ... this seeker turned her troubles into songs for us.

—Kim Stafford, author of *Early Morning: Remembering My Father, William Stafford*

Ronda Miller's understanding of the natural world is real and never glossed. So too, her people live in a Kansas of the heart, one with the wind that buffets them, a poetry that runs deep with a melancholy longing....

—Al Ortolani, author of *Paper Birds Don't Fly*

..,within her poetry, sacred word for eternity, she heals herself and is reborn.

—Xánath Caraza, award winning author of the International Latino Book Awards and author of *Syllables of Wind/Sílabas de Viento*

Ronda Miller's poems seek words to help us come to terms with all that life presents, and in the end, finds them.

—Roy Beckemeyer, author of *Music I Once Could Dance To* (2014, Coal City Press)

Ronda Miller's poetry is explosive and exceptional. She says 'if you want to know a poet, read his words...until they become your own.'

—Alan S. Kleiman, author of *Grand Slam*